THE HEARTSPACE PORTAL

MARK L COLLINS (SRIMAN DAS)

Publisher's Information

EBookBakery Books

Author contact: srimandas@gmail.com

ISBN 978-1-938517-64-8

© 2017 by QuantumLove.net

ALL RIGHTS RESERVED

ACKNOWLEDGMENTS

Viewable at: http://www.quantumlove.net/gurusamavaya.html

DEDICATION

To Jackson, my son, friend, and fellow tender of souls.

THE HEARTSPACE PORTAL

The day science begins to study nonphysical phenomena, it will make more progress in one decade than in all the previous centuries of its existence.
–Nikola Tesla

Physical is a small happening. In this cosmos, not even two percent, or not even one percent is physical, rest is non-physical.
 –Sadhguru

It is you that pervades this universe, and this universe exists in you. Your true nature is pure consciousness.
–Ashtavakra Gita

PREFACE

The goal of this book is to help you on your journey of finding who you really are, why you are alive, and what this life really is all about. As you read the story about my search for a deeper level of truth, which lies beyond the confines of science or religion, you will sense that I have found a wispy essence of something magical and profound. I believe that secret magical something is divine love, what I call the fabric of heaven, which is accessible to us all via the sacred space of the heart.

Regarding the book title, *Heartspace Portal* just rolled of my tongue one day when one of my dearest friends asked me what the name of my first book would be. I thank you dear friend for being so true, so loving, and so understanding and supportive; as you know, the great Goddess has blessed us both.

TABLE OF CONTENTS

1

WHAT FORMS THIS WORLD

This book touches on the story of my lifelong spiritual quest and the answers that have been revealed to me. I have found unifying and comforting answers to the mystery of our existence coming from modern science, ancient texts, spiritual belief systems and the ideas of great swamis, saints, shamans, and philosophers. My purpose is to share deeply insightful spiritual gems and pearls of philosophic wisdom regarding the nature of reality, both physical and metaphysical.

Some words, phrases and ideas are repeated throughout the book, for these are topics and concepts that I hope you will remember. The repetition is purposeful and will help you absorb and assimilate the ideas.

As you read this book you will discover the major themes discussed include:

↪ The oneness of consciousness which supports the idea of the interconnection of all life everywhere.

↔ The need for Western civilization to return to a veneration of God's other half, the Goddess. I call this the divine feminine Shakti force as it should really be thought of as an energy, rather than a personality.

↔ Recent theories of quantum physics are starting to resonate with ancient mystical teachings, especially those found in Vedic lore.

↔ A global transformation of consciousness is upon us, as we return to an awareness of the existence of metaphysical, higher dimensional levels of existence, which our physical reality is just a reflection of.

↔ That heart-based consciousness is the key to the healing and transformation of ourselves and therefore the entire world.

Up until I was 4 or 5 years old, I saw glimpses through the veil into the other worlds. I had retained an awareness of my eternal presence on the other side - another part of me that always did and will always exist.

I vaguely recall that other children, and some adults, would look at me quizzically when I tried to explain these visions. I explained that I knew what was "behind everything" - that I could see the vibration, the geometric forms, the energies of the higher dimensional essence that were the means by which things arose into existence.

It is only in recent years that I am now able to explain what I was seeing - the workings of energy, vibration, and sacred geometry via multiple levels of causation that emanates into this world to become the temporary substance we call matter.

I have been able to once again reconnect to some of that knowingness, or what I call higher dimensional awareness. Over there, all things are one. Everything happens at once, anything is possible, and it all exists in an ocean of divine love and peace.

The reason we cannot see and interact with the higher realms is that there is a void between dimensional levels. Some people have more ability than others to see through or receive information through the void.

However, the increase in our spiritual and psychic abilities is accelerating across the globe. We, as a species, are going to re-awaken to a multidimensional awareness where we will once again see right into the higher worlds, hopefully in the time of our current generation.

This expanded consciousness, a higher level awareness that is always present, exists within all of us. We are all aware of it as children, but the world seems to shut us off from it as we grow older. Most likely, the emotional jolts we receive from negative experiences in this world take us away from our quiet center. These harsh emotional experiences cause a separation from the voice of spirit.

This happened to me during my early childhood years. Nothing hugely traumatic, but these harmful events were enough to disconnect me from that peaceful internal state of knowing and higher level awareness.

It seems as we grow older and become adults, we become more caught up in the trappings of this existence.

By the time I was in my early teens, I was becoming more engrossed in material gratification in the world. I also began experimenting with some drugs and engaging in heavy social drinking.

Although my connection with the other side faded, I somehow was able to keep a spiritual perspective, and thankfully, I held on to my intense longing to study mystical spirituality.

Through my teens and college years I led a double life. I worked hard and partied hard, but I also read, studied metaphysics, and participated in various spiritual pursuits. By the time I was in my late 20s, I had become very career oriented and started to lose my spiritual center as I spent more and more hours working. A side benefit of this intense materialistic focus was that I stopped drinking and partying out of fear of losing my worldly success.

Addiction is a prevalent problem in our society, as it offers the illusion of escape from the uncomfortable aspects of our existence. For me, I became addicted to alcohol because it reduced my anxiety, which had its roots in my unhappiness about the more negative events and possibilities that exist in this world. I was lucky to find my way into a 12-step recovery program, which allowed me to put down the drink and get back to a spiritual focus in my life.

I can now honestly say that the best high I have experienced - and you can too - is the incredible peace and tranquility found in just a single moment of non-thought. In that space between the thoughts, we can connect with a higher awareness that exists beyond the body and mind, time and space. This experience has been described as a glimpse of heaven, a sensation of no time, omniscient awareness, omnipresence, or the feeling of being one with creator. To me, it is the greatest experience we can attain in this life.

I have only felt a connection with this higher realm of pure conscious awareness for a few fleeting instances, but those moments seemed eternal and peaceful. This experience provided me with a spirituality that allowed me to become more content and accepting of everything, while functioning normally in the real world and being unmoved by positive or negative circumstances (to the best of my ability).

Being aware of the heavenly realms (absolute reality) provides me with insights and inspiration to live a better life here in the physical world (temporal reality). This type of practically minded spirituality is what the world needs to narrow the divide between rationalism and spiritualism.

I have been deeply inspired by the words of Jeff Brown, author of *Soulshaping*, who wrote:

> *I am not interested in enlightenment if it means detachment from the emotional body, the earth plane, the challenges of being human. I am interested in enrealment, because it means that my most spiritual moments are inclusive, arising right in the heart of all that is human: joy and sorrow, shopping list and unity consciousness, fresh mangoes and stale bread. Enrealment is about living in all aspects of reality simultaneously rather than only those realms that feel the most comfortable. We are not just the light, or the mind, or the emptiness, or perpetual positivity. We are the everything. It's ALL God, even the dust that falls off my awakening heart.*

Up until my early 40s, I had achieved a reasonable amount of economic success, but I was becoming increasingly anxious, depressed, and somehow disconnected from the rest of the world. A good case of Lyme disease served to exacerbate the emptiness and depression I was feeling, so I began studying philosophy, metaphysics, and anything and everything I could get my hands on about spiritual knowledge. I then had my first exposure to Reiki. After receiving my first healing session, I immediately signed up to learn more and got my Reiki 1 certificate.

This was the beginning of a major shift. From this point on, my study of spirituality and metaphysics accelerated, and soon my house was filled with books on all matters metaphysical, spiritual, unexplained, and even paranormal. I did my best to balance my spiritual world with my work-a-day world by devoting what free time I had to spiritual study and learning. A brief list of some of the many topics, belief systems, practices, teachers and authors that influenced my learning is provided at the end of this book.

One day, while working at my regular job, one of my friends (Lisa M.) invited me to dinner so I could meet her then husband, Ric Oliveira who was the editor of *TAPS Paramag*, a fan magazine for the popular television show, *Ghost Hunters*. I am graciously indebted to them both, for she had described me as the "quintessential New Age guy" to him, just when he wanted to add a regular section to the magazine called the "Spirituality Almanac." He was willing to consider me to be the columnist, we hit it off, and I ended up writing the column for over five years. I then moved on to write the "Metaphysical View" column for *Intrepid Magazine,* captained by the inimitable Scotty Roberts, where I wrote for another three years.

In both of these columns I analyzed and summarized spiritual and metaphysical information from ancient and modern belief systems from around the world. I also co-hosted *The HeArt of Healing* radio show, now podcast on BlogTalk.com with Laura Mayer, author of *Unlocking The Invisible Child: A Journey from Heartbreak to Bliss*. Laura entered my life at a time when I needed a boost of confidence in my spiritual self. Her feedback, guidance, and support motivated me to finally start writing this book.

2

It Is All One

In the unitary, undifferentiated still ocean of Existence-Aware-
ness-Self, body, senses, mind, intellect and jivas (embodied souls)
are nothing but evanescent ripples not apart from that sole Self.
-From the *Ribhu Gita*

At some point during my spiritual quest, I started to keep a dream journal and noticed that I was having some precognitive experiences of future events. One day in early 2003, I wrote in my journal, "We are seated in a circle with the master at UMass. He said to us, 'You shall not attain enlightenment unless you meditate with me for at least 21 days straight.'"

Shortly thereafter, my Reiki master called and excitedly informed me that Guruji Swami Shree Yogi Satyam would be coming from his ashram in Allahabad, India, to nearby UMass Dartmouth. When I walked into the room at the Center for Indic Studies and sat down, the first thing he said was "you must attend Sadhana¹ with me for at least 21 days if you are sincerely seeking enlightenment and desire to experience a direct connection with creator."

I was deeply moved by his words, as it sounded so very similar to my dream. When I saw his face, I knew instantly he was the spiritual master I had encountered in the dream state. I attended Sadhana daily for the full 21 days that he was at UMass. It was life changing, as it started me on the path of meditation and inner discovery. As I look back, it took 11 years for his words and ideas to be absorbed fully into my being and for me to start trying to live them out in the real world.

In his teaching, Yogi Satyam implied that God realization is achieved when one totally accepts all aspects of the nature of our existence here in the physical universe. The key is to realize that things such as pain and pleasure are an immortal element of change. Thus, change itself is an expression of the omnipotent power of the creator - it is not to be protested, but accepted.

According to the Swami, "It is all one." There is no separation between us, the universe, or the Godhead. He implied that we need to accept life on life's terms and to work and function in the real world, while also devoting some time every day to being quiet and meditative. He said you do not need any religion or dogma or a particular God or Goddess to connect directly with creator.

All you have to do is sit quietly in a lotus position or any posture that keeps your spinal column straight. (Yogi Satyam calls the cerebrospinal system our "antenna to God.") It is most important to focus on breathing, for God is experienced through our breath. A focus on the sound, feeling, and movement of the breath will help alter your state of awareness and consciousness.

This technique, known as pranayama breathing allowed me to finally shut down my mind, which had always been racing and full of worries about the future or regrets about the past. But with the technique of focusing on the sensation and feeling of breathing, I was able to rise above my body and my mind to become aware once again of that higher level of consciousness that I once knew as a child - what he called omniscient, omnipresent awareness and what I describe as an awareness of the higher, nonphysical unseen dimensions or planes.

We are not ourselves; we are pure awareness, a consciousness that emanates from the higher nonphysical worlds of existence beyond the confines of time and space. This idea is supported by recent studies of near death experiences, which seem to have revealed that awareness can exist outside the body and brain.

> *You do not have a soul....You are a soul. You have a body temporarily.*
> -**Walter Miller**

To me, the crown jewel, the perfect pearl of spiritual wisdom, is that we can all connect directly with creator, that our consciousness is part of the consciousness of creator, and that we are therefore all connected to each other and all beings. Most importantly, we can achieve a state of complete inner bliss and happiness, regardless of our worldly condition and affairs, by going within and meditating to connect with the one-source consciousness. Loving creator directly allows you to love yourself, which then leads you to being able to love all beings and all things.

I believe that we all have the capacity to bring divine love energy into this world. In fact, it is our spiritual responsibility as sentient beings.

While I had initially embraced the New Age movement almost like an escape or opiate to distract myself from my inner angst, it served me well to mix and match belief systems, ideas, and spiritual concepts of who we are and why we are alive. This allowed me to open up my mind and transcend previously held, preconceived ideas and beliefs about the nature of reality.

Now, after realizing that we are really pure consciousness itself, I no longer need to seek or search for anything. I felt that I had finally found an answer to the riddle of creation itself, why we exist and what we really are.

Indeed, new quantum physics theories suggest that physical reality is not all there is. Other hidden dimensions or unseen vibrational levels seem to be affecting this one.

When you die, you may or may not retain your personality or an awareness of it. However, you are not the "you" you think you are - you are something incalculably greater.

This may seem paradoxical, but the great realization uncovered by the mystic masters is that the creator is shifting into us, temporarily, to experience itself. We are not really completely this consciousness, for we are also an aspect of a greater unified non-corporeal awareness. Those who are weak-minded or selfish might ask, "If our very existence is so fleeting, why should I work? Why should I live a moral life?"

Well, we have been given a huge responsibility, as creator is experiencing life through us. We are here to learn lessons from our experience of ordinary life, as the universal consciousness immerses itself completely into all forms, manifestations, and experiences of this reality. In this realm we have free will in our experience of duality, the separation of good and evil, black and white, and yin and yang. Our experiences work to evolve our consciousness, which in turn evolves the consciousness of the all-unifying self or super soul.

For example, we learn that some forms of competition can bring separation and that cooperation brings oneness and mutual success. And yet, another paradox is revealed when we realize that our moments of separation increase the joy of togetherness. We learn the hard lessons that abject service to self leads to emptiness and unhappiness. An excess of, food, material possessions, drugs, or sex never brings any real, lasting happiness. Indeed, too much of anything is likely to bring emotional pain, as intense attachment eventually brings suffering. And yet some of these things are needed to expand our consciousness, and most are not harmful if experienced in moderation.

Listening to the words of hospice patients as they lie on their deathbeds, all they talk about is their relationships and their feelings of joy and regret resulting from their connection to others. They almost never discuss their material possessions or worldly career achievements, and they certainly do not reflect positively on addictions or obsessions they had.

Our present society has us loving things more than people or animals and this earth. Now is time to realize that love and relationships are the pure gold that we should be seeking in this life. Love is the spiritual currency that we take with us through eternity when we leave the body and depart from this physical plane.

The illusion that we are "just physical" is the source of our disconnection from the godhead - and worse, from each other - as this belief prevents us from reflecting on the truth that we are actually metaphysical beings, temporarily manifesting into solid form. Physicality is not the center of creation, rather, it is the furthest extension or projection of nonphysical worlds and planes that are so infinite that our finite human minds cannot even begin to comprehend what they are.

Consciousness could well be creating this reality, and it may be the source of all matter. It could be what existed before the reality that we know and what will exist after. This is why some Eastern masters have called the physical universe "solidified consciousness."

The riddle of creation really appears to have been solved - that this reality is all a big thought.

Yogi Satyam stated that we are each but a thought in the mind of creator, that we are really a reflection, or a point of view, of that one universal, trans-dimensional consciousness. This revelation was very comforting to me because it implies that we do not dissolve into nothing at death; rather, we expand into everything.

> *"There exists only ONE Consciousness, which is called Omnipresent, Omnipotent, Omniscient, and Immortal. Nothing exists other than this. You, me, and everything we perceive is a manifestation of the Immortal Consciousness."*
> **-Guruji Swami Shree Yogi Satyam**

I have had several other precognitive experiences during my life, and they have served to validate some spiritual experience or lesson for me. The most profound spiritual experience of my life occurred when I was eight years old. One day, while looking at some books on a bookshelf, a white star flew out of one of the books and materialized a few feet in front of my face. It was as small as a pea but very bright. After it appeared, it swung around my head and then dove into my left ear. As it entered my head, I heard a chime sound, like a bell, and then my whole being, body, and mind felt supremely happy, peaceful, and filled with a good energy that I can only describe as pure joy. Only now do I understand that it was divine gift, a white spark of God energy, an initiation to enlighten me to my true purpose in this life. My mission is simply to remind you that the light and love of prime creator are very real and available to us all for the betterment of ourselves and this world.

The Deeksha Movement

Sri Kalki Bhagavan, founder of the Oneness University in India, developed a spiritual practice called the Deeksha blessing to achieve this very purpose. The Deeksha movement has expanded rapidly in the last two decades and is being practiced all around the world. Bhagavan describes the importance of the spiritual practice of Deeksha as follows:

"The Oneness Blessing (or Deeksha) is a Divine blessing that accelerates our movement toward awakening to oneness. It's a phenomenon of pure grace."

The foundational assertion of the World Oneness Movement is that an instantaneous transformational power is now available to all practitioners and recipients of the Deeksha blessing as enough "accelerated awareness" has been achieved in a critical mass of its followers worldwide. The attainment of Deeksha is further defined as the moment when one comprehends the ultimate truth, which results in freedom (moksha) from the cycle of karma (and reincarnation). The founding principle of the movement is that bestowing the Deeksha blessing is a way to transmit divine energy from person to person. Bhagavan predicted that this will lead to the attainment of total enlightenment, globally, within the next decade - or sooner.

In the Buddhist tradition, the goal of dedicated spiritual practice is to become a bodhisattva, or enlightened being. A compassionate devotion to this enlightened state is required on behalf of all sentient beings in the cosmos because it is thought that our spiritual vibrations affect all other sentient beings who reside in manifest creation.

This relates to another Buddhist concept called mindfulness, where we are not only required to take the right action on behalf of self and others but also to be mindful of actions we don't take and to reflect on the consequences that follow from failing to act.

While focusing on action and non-action is important, it is our reactions to people, places, and things in the world that are more likely to generate negative karma. This is why the current Dalai Lama, Tenzin Gyatso, said, "You can only change your universe by changing your reaction to it."

Once, we attain a bodhisattva state, we realize that our actions and reactions affect everyone's reality, as our minds and souls are connected in this world and also in the higher realms.

This Body Says

One of the greatest mystics to have lived in the last century was Anandamayi Ma, a living saint from Vrindavan, India. The life and teachings of Anandamayi, also known as "Ma," served to highlight the realization of the temporary nature of human selfhood. It was said that Ma always referred to herself only in the third person, calling herself "this body" or "this little daughter of yours." When people visited her ashram, she would explain to them that by coming to meet her they were simply coming to meet their own self. She would then say in parting "you are everything." In her Darshana, (a blessing given during spiritual teaching), Ma was known to have said:

I realized that the Universe was all my own manifestation....
I found myself face to face with the One that appears as many.

Ma's deep insight was the realization that while we may be in this world, we are not really of it, and that we all share the same divine essence at the core of our being. In the affairs of our day-to-day life, if we can honor the present divinity that resides within everyone, this awareness will bring cooperation, harmony, and peace to ourselves and to the world at large. We will leave behind the old paradigm of duality consciousness, which is based on the illusion of separateness, division, competition, and fear, and we can all start living the meaning of the ever popular Sanskrit phrase Namaste, which means:

The God spirit within me recognizes and honors the God spirit
within you.

13

The phrase "it is all one" has been conveyed by many spiritual masters, who have realized the wholeness of all creation to be the manifest, the un-manifest, and the infinite as part of the ever present "now." I have read this is why, in Hinduism, the number 108 is greatly significant, it is the recommend number of repetitions of a mantra, when chanted using mala beads: 1 represents the manifest, 0 represents the un-manifest, leaving 8 which represents infinity.

We are living in the time when we need to realize our oneness and interconnection, as we have all created everything together and are equally responsible for the positive and negative energy and events that exist in the world today. For what we think is "out there" in the world is really emanating from and living within us. We have become stuck in the limiting belief that what we perceive with our senses is a "reality" based on our experience, instead of taking responsibility for our creation of the experience in the first place. The book *A Course in Miracles* is clear on this point as it implies that this reality is a collective agreement, while also pointing out that when you strike down your brother you really are striking down yourself.

And if the un-manifest and manifest are connected, we should recall the Hermetic phrase, "As above so below, as within so without," to realize that as soon as we can all achieve total inner peace and oneness within it will manifest in the world - and as soon as that occurs heaven will return to earth.

3

God Is Right Under Your Nose

That which knows the body-mind is an awareness called the higher self, which really is a merging with the all-pervasive self or the one-source consciousness.

Meditative practice using pranayama breathing is an effective technique for quieting the mind. For it is in the moments of being breathless that we start to become "thought-less."

The way out is within. The secret to enlightenment is right under your nose, literally, as the life force, which is God energy, source energy, and the presence of creator - it resides in your breath. The breathless space between your inhalation and exhalation is where you connect to higher consciousness and awareness, per the words of the great Yogananda:

> *...breathlessness is the higher state of realization known as Samadhi (perfect union with God). We cannot perceive Truth until we have attained full mastery over breath.*

Samadhi[2] allows us to attain the mental state of omniscient awareness that the great master Sri Aurobindo called Supramental Consciousness. It is only when we achieve this state of awareness that we can start to feel the all-powerful love of creator. It is a feeling so profound that the mystics say human words cannot really be used to fully describe it.

I believe we can bring this blissful divine energy back into this world. In the sacred space of the heart, we can find a refuge where thoughts cease, allowing us to feel, not think, and allowing us to be, not do. In Gregg Braden's book, *The Isaiah Effect*, he studied Tibetan monks and learned that they do not manifest reality from intense thought or visualization. They focus only on the feeling of how they will feel when a particular state of being is achieved. Feelings, not thoughts, are far more important.

How we feel, vibrate, and resonate is the primary attracting force leading us to our experiences here in this reality. So how do we create or amplify those good feelings? We ask that the divine love of creator enter our hearts so that we can then infuse it into the world for the greatest good of all. We know that the gift offered by religion is unconditional love, which is a great healing and unifying force in our society and world. However, as spiritual beings, we are part of and connected to the one universal, trans-dimensional self.

We have the unique ability to access the highest form of love, which is divine love, or what I call Quantum Love. Also known as the Om Prema (Sanskrit for: divine love of creator), it flows directly from the Godhead into the world from the higher dimensions via the sacred space of the heart, or what I call the Heartspace Portal.

According to recent, popular interpretations of the law of attraction, we can create our own reality, as human consciousness has been shown to affect material reality at the quantum level. However, I believe it is more accurate to say that at an individual level we can influence our reality and, therefore, affect and impact the collective reality.

When we band together and vibrate into one loving, unified consciousness, only then will we "create" a new collective reality and a new world.

Feeling compassion, caring, love, and similar emotions has a powerful effect on both the individual and the greater population. Scientists at the HeartMath Institute now believe that a feedback loop exists between the planet and all living creatures. This is called the people-planet connection. The earth's magnetic resonances vibrate at the same frequency as human heart rhythms and brain waves. This field acts in synergy with the emotional energy that is fed into it. As the saying goes, "garbage in garbage out." That is why it is so important to be mindful of the emotions we choose to send into this field. It is believed that a relatively small number of participants, feeling positive emotions, are needed to reach a critical mass that would have a profound influence on the greater population subconsciously. This is why it is important to maintain individual peace and harmony, as we are all connected to the same, unified field of intent.
www.glcoherence.org for more information.

4

Thou Art That

The following phrases are the headline of my website:
Tat Tvam Asi,
In Lakech ala Kin,
Ola Lokahi,
Ubuntu,
Ehyeh Asher Ehyeh,
Namaste,
Mitakuye Oyasin

Each phrase roughly translates to the same thing: **We are one with each other, it is all one.**

Once we detach from ego and let go of the I, we become conscious of the "am." The Egyptians described our spiritual being as having two parts; The *ba*, which is the mental or personal life force, and the *ka*, which is the spirit, or essence of the oversoul. We cannot find blissful peace and contentment until we connect with the "am," the *ka*, or what we call the higher self. Although we each have an individuated consciousness, we must realize our oneness with each other and with Creator - for everything is connected, and we are all part of a larger super soul that unites all beings.

> *We spend 99.9 percent of our time trying to bring happiness to our self, the problem is, there isn't one. Ask the awakened.*
> -**Andrea Tteja**[3]

The ancient Mayan saying, *In Lak'ech Ala K'in*, means: *I am another you, I am that which you also are.* It implies that you and I are "that," i.e., extensions or expressions of the I AM presence, which is a higher, inter-connected consciousness. In short, "that" is the "am" of the "I am" awareness. If that is the "over soul," and you and I are "that," then we are all part of a collective consciousness that is so great that our minds can barely comprehend it.

In the ancient Vedic lore of the Upanishads, we find a similar quote, *Tat Tvam Asi* that also means *thou art that,* the knower of the body mind, or that which observes. Brahman: Chandogya *Upanishad* 6.8.

Likewise Deepak Chopra expressed the idea of the oneness of our consciousness when he said:

> *I am not a mind in a body, I am a body in a great big mind.*

Nonduality

In the history of modern spiritual thought, Meher Baba[4], another great spiritual philosopher from India, popularized nonduality. This metaphysical concept implies that duality, or the separateness of all forms of creation, is an illusion as the God force is actually inherent in all matter, whether living or inanimate. This stems from his description of God's original state as an infinite ocean of unconscious divinity, which was unaware of its own existence.

God then became self aware and asked *Who am I?* Creation itself then came into existence as the resulting answer to God's question. As the ocean broke apart, it formed into individual parts of itself, or - these fragments are our souls. Each soul has inherited the same desire for self-knowledge as the creator. This is why the yogis say that the path of self-realization leads to God realization.

Baba's further discourse on spiritual mechanics includes the intriguing concept of "spiritual evolution" where each individual soul-entity reincarnates successively through all forms of "conscious matter," i.e., stone, vegetable, worm, fish, bird, animal, and human. Through this process, the conscious awareness of the entity slowly expands as the impressions of each existence is imprinted upon it, until an awareness of its own divinity is achieved through the eons of time and existence.

Once a soul enters the human form, it can begin its pursuit of an inner spiritual path of which the final goal is to know itself as a conscious part of divinity is attained. Finally, the soul entity can merge back into the "ocean" of God. Like other eastern mystics, Meher Baba explains that the answer to the ultimate question, *Who am I?* is answered with *I am God.*

Spirituality, meditation, and inner reflection lead us to a glimpse of fifth-dimensional (5-D) consciousness, where there is no need to create or act. 5-D is a state of awareness, which is unified with all that is, was, or ever will be, in all dimensions and all realities. All we need to do is just shift our awareness to experience the state of internal being that we desire. The gift of fifth-dimensional awareness is that it makes us realize that heaven can be right here with us all now, for again, there is no separation.

5

SWAMIS & SCIENTISTS

The New Age was a grafting of new ideas onto old models and a mixing and matching of diverse spiritual beliefs. This was a positive shift in our spiritual evolution. But now, with the proof of nonphysical planes of existence so near, we are truly living in the Great Age.

Modern-day science had caused us to view the underlying fabric of the universe as dead, inert building blocks. But now, a new movement in science is asserting that a field of infinite possibility is emanating from the zero-point vacuum of space time. I believe that this vacuum, or void, is the source of an ethereal consciousness that forms, shapes, and molds matter into existence.

Fritjof Capra, a physicist and author of *The Tao of Physics: An Exploration of the Parallels Between Modern Physics and Eastern Mysticism,* came to realize through his study of physics at the quantum level that the Eastern metaphysical concepts at the core of his spiritual beliefs coincided almost perfectly with the laws of quantum mechanics. This led to his concept that an all-unifying force organizes all matter, *there are hidden connections between everything.*

A similar idea of an unseen force was echoed by David Bohm, a physicist and contemporary of Capra. Bohm theorized that while there was a concrete provable "explicate order" of matter and creation, he felt that an "implicate order" had to exist, where a "hidden influence that organizes existence" was also present.

According to Bohm, this influence "resonates from an energy field which is yet greater, the realm of pure potential. It is pure potential because nothing is implied within it: implications form in the implicate order, and then express themselves in the explicate order."

Many ancient cultures knew of this unifying force, which in Vedic lore is described as one all-pervasive being, Brahman, which caused reality to manifest as an interconnected web or matrix of all matter. David Bohm regularly corresponded with the Indian philosopher Jiddu Krishnamurti. In the 1960's, Krishnamurti told Bohm that the universe was expanding, even though theoretical physicists of the time firmly believed the universe was finite. Expansion is now part of modern quantum theory.

Recent discoveries regarding space and the wave form structure of matter confirm that all things are interconnected; from the empirical scientific view, *subatomic particles have no meaning as isolated entities but can only be understood as interconnections between the preparation of an experiment and the subsequent measurement.*

This means that as we try to break matter down to its smallest parts, nature does not reveal itself as finite, solid "basic building blocks," but rather, as a web of complex relations that exist between the parts and the whole.

According to the Tesla Society, Nikola Tesla was influenced by the Vedic philosophy teachings of Swami Vivekananda. And, Erwin Schrödinger's formulation of quantum theory was affected by his study of the metaphysical aspects of Vedanta, a principal branch of Hindu philosophy. He said: *The unity and continuity of Vedanta are reflected in the unity and continuity of wave mechanics. This is entirely consistent with the Vedanta concept of All in One.*

Prior to 1925, physics assumed that the universe was a machine-like structure comprised of separate, material particles that interact. Schrödinger and Nikola Tesla developed a new quantum theory paradigm of the universe based on inseparable waves of probability amplitudes that coexist. This new idea supported the Vedantic concept that all is one and the view that physical reality is created by, and dependent upon, an all-unifying, unseen force.

Looking further at the parallels between quantum physics and Vedic information, we find that Bohm's description of the "ground of existence" sounds very similar to the great Indian philosopher Swami Vivekananda's explanation of what the Hindu's call the Akasha:

It is the omnipresent, all-penetrating existence. Everything that has form, everything that is the result of combination, is evolved out of this Akasha. It is the Akasha that becomes the air, that becomes the liquids, that becomes the solids; it is the Akasha that becomes the sun, the earth, the moon, the stars, the comets; it is the Akasha that becomes the human body, the animal body, the plants, every form that we see, everything that can be sensed, everything that exists. It cannot be perceived; it is so subtle that it is beyond all ordinary perception; it can only be seen when it has become gross, has taken form. At the beginning of creation there is only this Akasha. At the end of the cycle the solid, the liquids, and the gases all melt into the Akasha again, and the next creation similarly proceeds out of this Akasha.[5]
-Swami Vivekananda

What we perceive through the senses as empty space is actually the plenum, which is the ground for the existence of everything, including ourselves. The things that appear to our senses are derivative forms and their true meaning can be seen only when we consider the plenum, in which they are generated and sustained, and into which they must ultimately vanish." In contemporary science space is rediscovered as the fundamental matrix in which the manifest things and events of the universe arise, in and through

which they evolve, and into which they again redescend.[5]
-David Bohm

Also, in this reference from the Upanishad's, we find an explanation of the Akasha that reflects Bohm's idea of the explicate and implicate order.

> *The Akasha is not merely one element among others; it is the fundamental element: the ultimately real dimension of the cosmos. It is what in its subtle aspect underlies all things and in its gross aspect becomes all things. In its subtle aspect it cannot be perceived. But it can be observed in its gross aspect, in which it has become the things that arise and evolve in space and time…. 'All beings arise from space, and into space they return: space is indeed their beginning, and space is their final end.*
> *-Chandogya Upanishad* I.9.1[5]

Another way to view the explicate and implicate would be as the Prakriti,(matter) and Purusha (spirit).

As for the all-unifying force that quantum physicists are searching for, author David Wilcock said, *The underlying fabric of the universe is consciousness…waves and particles are not separate things.*

Akin to David Wilcock's statement, Dr. Amit Goswami[6], a physics professor from the University of Oregon, also believes that *consciousness is the ground of being.*

Similarly in the 1700s, Ralph Waldo Emerson's Transcendentalist idea of God was that one source maintained and animated all life in the whole cosmos along with the human soul. Emerson wrote that *God is the substratum of all souls* and that *the Soul is the kingdom of God, the abode of love, of truth, of virtue.*

Theosophists, transcendalists, and universalists all viewed God as an unchanging, infinite, transcendent reality and a divine ground of all beingness. Goswami, who was featured in the movie *What the Bleep Do We Know?*, calls himself the Quantum Activist. In an interview on Coast to Coast AM radio, Goswami explained that he is re-examining materialism, which he says is really only a 50-year-old phenomenon. He says that before materialism we had dualism, where mind and matter were connected in a self-aware universe. His goal is to discover how consciousness creates the material world.

Goswami talked about the science within consciousness, and how the paradigm is shifting from a materialistic world view to one that incorporates spirituality and the mystic traditions. He believes that *the existence of God is being revealed in the signature of quantum physics.*

In Goswami's view, if quantum physics says every object is a possibility, then there has to be a nonmaterial entity that chooses the actual event from the process of these possibilities. He explains that in quantum physics, there is also the concept of non-locality, a signal-less communication outside of space and time. Goswami says these communications could be mediated by an all-unifying consciousness and that this possibility relates to religious notions of God.

Goswami feels that the materialist viewpoint tends to be pessimistic as it doesn't find value or meaning in the simple beauty and magnificence of manifest creation. He urges us to become connoisseurs of consciousness, so that we can all begin to understand that we are more than just material bodies. He says we have a vital body which feels, and the coupling of this vital energy with the physical organ gives us vitality. Only when this coupling is weakened, do we then fall sick or out of harmony with our true life's purpose.

Goswami foresees humankind evolving over the next centuries, integrating emotions and thought in a more balanced way, saying that "people will learn how to harness the energies of love and access more of the intuitive mind."

Goswami's premise is that in the world of quantum physics: *the totality of all the anomalous data adds up to something that can be explained.*

After integrating Goswami's scientific insights about the possibility of hidden, non-physical realms with everything I have learned from spiritual mystics, my goal is to now remind you that you are cosmic consciousness. I want to take you out of your body, off the earth, and into the higher planes through meditative practice so that you can realize you need to live a spiritually minded life and understand that gaining knowledge of absolute reality gives us the tools to better experience and navigate temporal reality here on earth. Why? Because it makes us realize our complete interdependence.

Utopia will only be achieved by working together. I feel the only reason we do not yet have utopia is that most of us, including myself at times, have been walking the earth in a metaphysical stupor imprisoned by a limited understanding of the total nature of reality.

We are a bio-holographic projection of divinity, a reflection
or slice of a higher transdimensional consciousness and being.
- **Dr. Leonard G. Horowitz**

The paradox of life is to know that this world could be just a temporary illusion, created by the all-pervasive consciousness, and yet this life is also a great and precious gift that must savored and lived out with the fullest rationality, with our feet on the ground, with our eyes open, and with love for ourselves and compassion for others. The best fruits of this life often come from hard work, service, and love of our fellow humans and creatures.

However, it is not the material possessions and worldly successes that we reflect upon on our deathbeds; it is our relationships with others, ourselves, and creator that we focus on just before passing back into spirit. The value of metaphysical reflection is that it gives us both comfort and inspiration to accept and deal with life's challenges and tests here in the physical.

It appears that many quantum physicists have been inspired by Vedic concepts. We can find an example of this in the concept of spiritual planes.

The Kybalion mentions the three great planes of existence as being the physical, mental, and spiritual levels. Hinduism also makes references to planes of existence, spiritual worlds, or abodes that are above and beyond the physical. In the spiritual teachings of Eckankar[7], a modern path based on ancient teachings, six levels of existence are defined as the Physical, Astral, Causal, Mental, Etheric, and Soul planes. Similarly, in Kabbalah, the stations of the tree of life represent emanations of creation from the heavenly realms into the lower worlds. In all of these sources, the higher spiritual planes have been described as nonphysical levels that have created this reality and are influencing it.

Also, because ancient India holds so much deep knowledge of metaphysics, with the swamis' ideas mirroring quantum physics so perfectly, the idea that humans have been on this earth a lot longer than we currently believe or have yet discovered. And the information found in Vedic lore could well be a remnant of knowledge from a previous unknown advanced human civilization. As archaeologist Graham Hancock said: *We are a civilization with amnesia.*

I had discovered from my study of various authors like Zecharia Sitchin, Robert Temple, and Laird Scranton that the ancient Sumerians recount the existence of human civilization on this Earth to at least 400,000 years ago. But Michael Cremo, author of *Human Devolution* (and many other great works), has been the most influential source for my expanded awareness. When I read his work showing detailed references in Vedic lore and discussing human civilization existing on earth a few million years to perhaps many millions of years, my mind (and ego) truly opened up to realizing how little we still know about the true history of humans as a galactic species.

The archaic revival is upon us, the time when we unify ancient information with modern knowledge to arrive at the real truth of our history and existence.

Modern quantum string theory references the idea that hidden dimensions or levels are affecting and forming the physical. This could mean that science is indeed on the verge of proving the reality of other dimensions or the higher spiritual planes (abodes).

6

BALANCING THE WORLDS

Reflecting on our metaphysical nature reminds us that we are part of the unified whole of all beings and all creation This leads us out of the despair that comes from the illusion that we are separate, a temporary ego/body/mind complex, and not the eternal soul.

At birth, we experience a higher-dimensional awareness but our worldly life disconnects us from the higher abodes. Due to societal conditioning, we often become completely unaware of our reason for being by the time we reach adulthood.

Many of us live under the illusion that we are all separate beings in a purely mechanical universe. As these illusions fade, the collective nature of consciousness comes to light. This consciousness is not only shared between humans, but with all things in the universe.
-Rupert Sheldrake

The Native American spiral glyph shows a line spiraling out from a center point in widening concentric circles from a central starting point to an end point at the widest circle. Some tribes believe that you spend the first half of your life spiraling out into the world from birth, immersing yourself into materiality to gain experiences and lessons until you reach the end point on the spiral.

Then, you take the spiraling journey in from the outer point to the center of the circle, back into yourself to reconnect with your true essence, your soul.

The Native American traditions teach us to see the web of all creation as one, yet the symbolic message of this spiral glyph is that we must embrace and experience the separate manifestations, forms, and conditions of life. Our interaction with people, places, activities, objects, and attachments are the source of life's lessons. Therefore, as many spiritual teachers have said, each person you meet on the path is a guru, as all are manifestations of the one God consciousness.

Wisdom is the oneness of things, compassion is the many-ness of things.
-DT Suzuki

Parodox of Being

The classic definition of metaphysics is that it is the study of the nature of reality and existence. If we look further, the word *meta* means beyond, and the word *physics* means the physical world; so *metaphysics* is really the study of what lies beyond matter. The origin of the word metaphysics implies that we must study what lies beyond or what occurs before reality.

When we reflect upon the ubiquitous phenomenon of consciousness, it has been traditionally defined as the ability to perceive something, which requires this "something" to reside outside of itself in order to function. The classic supposition is that in order to be, consciousness is dependent upon existence itself. But perhaps it is really the opposite. In that case: Who are we? What are we? Why are we alive?

We are all here to evolve consciousness itself and our individual mission is self-realization. Nirvikalpa Samadhi is defined by Swami Sri Yukteswar in *The Holy Science*, as being able *to realize the supreme reality behind all names and forms,* in other words, to discover that we are all that one true universal self.

Some of the newer versions of a unified theory of everything in quantum physics hint at the idea that an all-pervasive consciousness could be the source from which matter is formed. This implies that consciousness exists in the meta state; in short, consciousness comes before matter. Could this be possible?

> *I regard consciousness as fundamental. I regard matter as derivative from consciousness. We cannot get behind consciousness. Everything that we talk about, everything that we regard as existing, postulates consciousness.*
> **-Max Planck**

> *You have theories about how this consciousness is created. But they are invented after this consciousness is present.*
> **-Nisargadatta Maharaj**

> *You have never, for a fraction of a second, ceased being the presence of awareness – unlimited, ever-present awareness. You have never ceased to be that.*
> **-Rupert Spira**

There have been intriguing scientific experiments, like the double-slit which demonstrates that light and matter can be displayed either as waves or particles. The measurement problem, encountered in quantum physicists, repeatedly shows that the consciousness of the observer affects the outcome of the experiment. At the deepest core of physical reality, we encounter the quantum superstring, which has been described as the "field of infinite possibility" from which matter arises.

The discovery of the energy field we call the quantum superstring is so very positive, inspiring, hopeful, and reassuring to me. Why? It pushes aside the depressing, fatalistic assumptions that the universe and ourselves are merely the sum of mechanical parts; it affirms that at the basic core of reality, there seems to be a field of energy that is alive with light and vibration.

The unified field is non material so it is one consciousness…
The self is universal, discovering that is called enlightenment.
–Dr. John Hagelin

On a grand scale, there is a pattern and a flow of synchronicities and events in the world and in our lives. I feel the only explanation for this possibility is frequency and vibration, coming from a higher source that we are connected to and can tap into. If everything is connected to the one source consciousness, then the answer to why we are alive is that we are to evolve consciousness itself, while experiencing this life as an extension of creator.

Stay embodied and fluid, we are experience experiencing itself.…
there are millions of selves within the one self so let it unfold, go
with the flow. Go share your light and love in the world, you
don't have to be perfect, just listen to your conversation with the
universe. Holiness is found in our humanness. The supernatu-
ral is really just natural, we are hooked in already, just listen.
-Simran Singh

It has been said that when we leave our bodies at death and enter the higher worlds, we enter a level of awareness where there is no time and space, where all possibilities exist at once, and where all points of view are true, from each perspective. At death, we rejoin the field of infinite possibility which can really be thought of us a unifying and all powerful super-consciousness.

The great Indian philosopher Jiddu Krishnamurti said, "Freedom from the desire for an answer is essential to the understanding of a problem." He was addressing the need for the human ego mind to have everything solid and concrete and to cling to something definite, when in fact, everything in this universe is as temporary as it is finite.

As we contemplate the fleeting nature of our existence, the paradoxical nature of our being emerges. The un-manifest could be the true reality, and the temporal world is an illusion and just a temporary reflection of the higher dimensional, nonphysical heavenly worlds.

If consciousness is what connects the heavens with earth, then we can bring that higher awareness into the world through ourselves for the betterment of all creation.

7

THE MAGIC OF MOTHERHOOD

When I was 19 years old, I had a brief discussion about gender equality over dinner with my first girlfriend and her mother, who was a dynamic, open-minded, progressive thinker like my own mother. I admired her greatly, and she had raised a daughter who was equally intelligent and confident but also spiritually aware and intuitive.

Marcia's mom handed me a book, written by Ashley Montagu, called *The Natural Superiority of Women.* Montagu's book made total sense to me, as he described how, since the dawn of time, women were naturally revered for their ability to create life. As civilization advanced, female intuition and unconditional compassion also become indisputably powerful, magical qualities in the minds of men. For centuries, the Goddess reigned supreme as she represented survival of the species through procreation, creativity, love, and the vitality women gave to all aspects of day-to-day life.

According to Montagu, the real source of female superiority is spiritual. He said:

> *Women are the carriers of the true spirit of humanity – the love of the mother for her child. The preservation and diffusion of that kind of love is the true function and message of women. And let me, at this point, endeavor to make it quite clear why I mean the love of a mother for her child and not the love of an equal for an equal, or any other kind of love.*

Mother Teresa said *we, too, must give to each other until it hurts*. As a young man, after pondering these two quotes, I finally understood that a mother gives just for the sake of giving, with no expectation of anything being returned, and even if it causes her pain. So, as Montagu said, the act of motherhood itself is the sacred spiritual function that allows our civilization to continue. Motherhood is the real power behind our survival as a species.

The average man needs to understand this - that selfless love is God-like; that it is really the most divine action we take as humans. Brotherly love is similar to romantic love in its devotion, however, divine love (the Om Prema) is the highest type of love we can describe. Om Prema incorporates something heavenly. The actions of a mother serve to sustain life by creating and nurturing souls, as they adapt to living in this world. A mother is indeed a conduit of the energy of divine love.

Mother as Gurudevi

I had a close relationship with my mother, as she was also my spiritual mentor. Although she has passed into spirit, this book was inspired partly by the conversations and beliefs she and I shared.

Almost all of the conversations, thoughts, and ideas we exchanged over four decades of time together were about spiritual matters. We both had the same goal of Moksha, which is an attainment of ascension while still in human form, an escape from the cycle of

Samsara (reincarnation). We also shared a belief in Meher Baba's concept of spiritual evolution, as part of the journey to self-realization or Nirvikalpa Samadhi that would lead us to God realization.

Touched by the Divine

Having studied and written about many of the belief systems, I began to fall in love with the Hindu pantheon of Gods and Goddesses. I was drawn to the ideal of the various emanations of divine mother, who is known by many names in the many Hindu paths. Adi Parashakti (Mahadevi) as Durga, Kali, Lakshmi, Parvati, Sati and Radha, which motivated me to try chanting mantras to divine mother. Over the course of time, the effect of the mantras began to open my heart, which then allowed me to become still and quiet enough to once again have spiritual experiences, like those I had experienced in my youth.

And then, a divine partnership arose when I was touched by a presence from the other side. On 9/2/2009 at 9:02 a.m., I looked out at my lawn and saw, reflected on the dew in the grass, the perfect image of the ancient Nordic rune, Gebo, which is written as an X. This rune symbolizes partnership, exchange, a gift. My logical mind traced the obvious cause of the X-shaped reflection to be from the frame of a window on the side of the house. However, it was centered perfectly within an egg-shaped sphere of light – a synchronicity, a coincidence. While this is a common light refraction occurrence, it was the sphere surrounding it formed by just the right angle of light streaming through the trees and reflecting on the morning dew, that astounded me. The perfection of the sphere with its intense brightness and the contrast of colors seemed miraculous as it hovered over the dew and changed the color of the dew to violet. As for the rune, the week before I had just completed studying the meanings of the Runic alphabet.

A few weeks later on 9/20/2009 at 9:20 a.m., after my daily mantras, I was reflecting on the experience of seeing the Gebo rune when I suddenly became aware of a divine presence. I felt a feeling of intense love flow down into my head and then into my heart. I would describe this sensation as undeniably powerful and real, a feeling sent from the higher realms.

I felt a loving, feminine hand touch my heart. I wept and shuddered. I even rolled on the floor the feeling was so intense. I can honestly attest that I have not ever been that moved; I have never felt anything that tender, that powerfully beautiful and divine.

I later realized that 9/20/2009 was the second day of Navratri that year, in celebration of the Goddess Brahmacharini, known as the one who grants Moksha. The hand felt like it was from the spirit of my departed mother; Moksha was our shared spiritual goal, and before she passed, the last spiritual discussion we had was about Moksha. My prayers to divine mother had brought me a reconnection to my mom. Brahmacharini had opened the veil for just an instant, just long enough for me to sense and know it was her spirit. It was undeniable given the profound physical, mental, and emotional effect it had on me.

In numerology, 0902009 and 09202009 are both 1111 dates, and the experiences occurred at 11 times (9:02 and 9:20), which I also found to be an interesting coincidence.

Sisters

Although my mother was the closest and most dearest to me in my life, my sisters played a large role in raising me since they were older and our parents both worked full time while juggling the demands of raising nine children. I believe that learning about the world from them helped me develop differently than most men, as I did not become a herd thinker. They really saw me for who I was, and their support gave me a boost spiritually.

Smithies

When I was a student at UMass-Amherst, I spent a lot of time socializing in the dorms at nearby Smith College, then a women's only school. I used to go every Wednesday night to watch TV with them; there would usually be fifteen young women and one or two other lucky guys present. A childhood friend of mine from sixth grade attended Smith, and she was gracious enough to invite me in to be with her dormitory friends.

To be in the vibrant presence of so many young woman of intellect no doubt helped me retain my childhood awareness of the goddess energy. I was allowed into their world, and I was able to ask and then hear what they thought and felt about the metaphysical at a time in my life when I was still receptive to that intuitive, knowing part of myself.

Having four older brothers, I also got a good dose of male enculturation. I played hockey; I worked in construction and on a commercial fishing boat; and I drank beer and watched football on the weekends like most other middle class men of my era.

Even with a healthy dose of strong female influence from my mother and sisters, I do, after all, have a male mind. And the way women think is just so fascinatingly different from how the male mind works that I always seem to learn new ways to look at things from them.

I would also like to clarify that it's not about being a sex, an age, or some other label to be able to become open-minded, intuitive and sensitive – it's about consciousness, being sentient, loving, good, and kind. To be a balanced being in both polarities of your own inner Shiva/Shakti. We need to adore each other and everyone, from a space of innocent, guileless, loving empathy. Each one of is such a miracle of creation, another potential God or Goddess with equal co-creative power.

To All the Women Who Have Loved Me

I am blessed to have had your love and for the lessons we learned from each other. I do realize I still have a long way to go to earn the grace of the great Goddess herself, just know that I am filled with gratitude for the association and good times we shared together. With your influence, love, and support, I feel I am getting closer to living relationships from a divine perspective as inspired by Baba's words:

The world as a whole has forgotten the real meaning of the word love. Love has been so abused and crucified by man that very few people know what true love is. Just as oil is present in every part of the olive, so love permeates every part of creation. But to define love is very difficult, for the same reason that words cannot fully describe the flavor of an orange. You have to taste the fruit to know its flavor. So with love.

Many human beings say "I love you" one day and reject you the next. That is not love. One whose heart is filled with the love of God cannot willfully hurt anyone. When you love God without reservation, He fills your heart with His unconditional love for all. That love no human tongue can describe.... The ordinary man is incapable of loving others in this way. Self-centered in the consciousness of "I, me, and mine," he has not yet discovered the omnipresent God who resides in him and in all other beings. To me there is no difference between one person and another; I behold all as soul-reflections of the one God.

In the universal sense, love is the divine power of attraction in creation that harmonizes, unites, binds together.... Those who live in tune with the attractive force of love achieve harmony with nature and their fellow beings, and are attracted to blissful reunion with God.
-**Meher Baba**

I do hope, dear women, to continue learning from Meher Baba's words. (Especially to my dear Jolie, you know who you are, and thank you for your enormous patience).

Humanity, particularly Western civilization, has lacked awareness of the manifestation of the one magical life-transforming energy we all possess, that alchemical power we call love, especially divine love. Thankfully, the Goddess energy is now returning to balance our society and world. My need to venerate her is ingrained in my soul.

I had once read a theory which proposed the interesting idea that the Fall of Rome resulted from Christianization because a disconnection from the Goddess resulted in our disconnection from nature and each other. In times past, northern Europeans, along with cultures all over the world, venerated her as the ultimate spiritual figure and an icon to be revered.

Unfortunately, patriarchal dominance and subjugation replaced cooperative interdependence. The rigidity of beliefs caused a separation of the heart from the mind and the great loss of the idea that spirit connects us all.

Medicine also suffered at hands of this mechanistic view, as we began to view ourselves as simply the sum of inanimate parts and not as a vital entity with interconnected systems, a soul, and spirit. Bernie Segal's *Love, Medicine and Miracles* re-opened the door to the idea that we may indeed be something more, and healing modalities like Reiki seem to be proving that unconditional love and positive intent have great power to help the mind and body to heal. Holistic, interconnected spirituality is the way home, where cooperation, love, and consideration for others is the key.

It may appear that another paradox exists between service to self versus service to others. We need to serve ourselves to survive as well as to experience and learn about the world. However, service to others can be a source of great joy, while also allowing for the survival and success of the whole. So again it's about balance, with unconditional love being the true mediator of these two necessary functions.

8

RETURN OF THE DIVINE FEMININE

The Great Goddess is the missing spiritual link for me, if not for our entire civilization, and I now know I have been seeking her my whole life. This book relays the story of my spiritual journey and the wisdom I have learned along the way; its purpose is to share what I have learned so that we may recognize and put into practice a renewed reverence for the divine feminine.

The goal of our existence, to my mind, is to gain spiritual wisdom and expand our capacity to love, as these two aims are inextricably linked and integral to the process of the unfoldment of consciousness. In other words, our purpose as spiritual beings, who are having a human experience, is to develop consciousness itself, guided by the energy of divine love.

The hopeful information revealed by some recent theories of quantum physics is allowing us to move out of the New Age and into what we should call the Great Age, when science finally proves the idea of higher, hidden dimensions of reality along with some of the larger, more pantheistic mystical tenets of spiritual belief.

Spiritually, if we balance our God image with the Goddess, we start to view the universe itself as being more loving, supportive, and creative.

So what of the Goddess? My whole life, I have felt there was something missing from our society, our culture, and from most of the religious information I have studied. The world just seemed to be out of balance to me. The most striking example of how we are disconnected from the Goddess has been our disconnection from the Earth Mother.

Vibrating Light Source Energy

Most folks only believe in what they experience through their five senses and deny their sixth sense. For them, I'd like to recall a quote from the great scientist Niels Bohr, who said:

> *Everything we call real is made of things that cannot be regarded as real.*"

This idea really hit home with me when I learned that at the subatomic level, we are not solid at all; we are actually 99.9999 percent empty space. The fact that matter is mostly not matter makes me think we are studying the wrong data set by focusing only on the .0001 percent of what is known as reality.

Srinivasa Ramanujan[8], a devout Hindu, had mathematical patterns revealed to him by the goddess Namagiri on his deathbed in 1920. In a letter to fellow mathematician, G. H. Hardy, his ideas described mysterious functions that mimicked theta functions, or modular forms. Like the trigonometric functions such as sine and cosine, theta functions have a repeating pattern, but the pattern is much more complex and subtle than a simple sine curve. Theta functions are also "super-symmetric," meaning that if a specific type of mathematical function called a Moebius transformation is applied to the functions, they turn into themselves. Because they are so symmetric these theta functions are useful in many types of mathematics and physics, including string theory.

When you read some of the more recent theories about the quantum superstring, which is the study of what lies at the most basic physical level of reality, it turns out that the smallest elements are described as a vibrating field of light energy waves. The idea is that all the subatomic particles and waves we have discovered are just different harmonics emanating from the quantum string field.

I found this to be so very hopeful, to know that the fabric of reality is alive with light and vibration. To me, the "loops of string" in this field are life-creating, like the divine feminine itself, as the shape of nothing - 0 - becomes everything when it 0 wiggles and twists to form - 8 - (infinite life). Or, as Kurt Vonnegut put it, to put it simply:

Everything is nothing, with a twist.
-Kurt Vonnegut

When I looked for a definition of string theory I found the following description from a course produced by the Science Media Group:

> *A The common element in all of these theories is that the fundamental objects are not point-like particles, but tiny strings that can form loops. The particles we normally think about correspond to vibrations of these loops of string.*[9]

Basically, the waves and particles that comprise matter arise from these strings.

The Goddess behind it all

In the ancient Hindu texts, the triad of the gods Brahma, Vishnu, and Shiva represent the three highest manifestations of the one reality. Yet, above and beyond these three, exists the Mahadevi, the great goddess or Shakti of all. Also known as the Adi Parashakti[10,] she is the power that underlies temporal reality.

Adi Parashakti supplies the Mulaprakriti, "that aspect of the Absolute which underlines all the objective aspects of Nature." (To clarify the previous mention of Akasha or the Akash, it is the first emanation of Mulaprakriti, so the Akasha and Mulaprakriti are closely related and very similar.) Adi Parashakti is the absolute source of reality itself and therefore the primal creative power (the word Shakti means power). One of her emanations is the formless creator of space:

Aditi (Adi Parashakti) is a sky goddess and mother of the gods "from whose cosmic matrix the heavenly bodies were born. As celestial mother of every existing form and being, the synthesis of all things, she is associated with space (Akasa) and with mystic speech (Vāc). She may be seen as a feminized form of Brahma and associated with the primal substance (Mulaprakriti) in Vedanta."

This concept, that the Prakriti is formed from the Purush, so the god creates via the energy of the goddess. Therefore, she could be very well be described as that which empowers the quantum superstring.

> **Note:** Shiva is one of the Trimurti, or triad of Gods. But as the Shiva/Shakti represents male/female polarity, Shiva also has a separate generic meaning.

In the Brahmanda Purana, it is stated that Mulaprakriti is the source from which all the divine goddesses emanated as Adi Parashakti, Durga, Lakshmi, Saraswati, Sita, Parvati, and Radha. In the Hindu world, Shaktism is one of the major paths of spiritual practice; Shaktism is the belief that the Shakti force is ultimate creator.

I am fond of using Hindu ideology because of the profound beauty of the Hindu Pantheon of Gods and Goddesses and because Sanskrit words and Vedic concepts exist which describe both spiritual ideas and scientific concepts quite efficiently. India holds great ancient knowledge. Proof of this is that it often takes many English words to describe a single Sanskrit word. Modern science has spawned the archaic revival, as it is revealing what the ancients knew.

Quantum Shaktism

At the quantum level, along with everything else in universe, we are vibrating waves of light emanating from the quantum superstring. I choose to view the quantum superstring as the Adi Parashakti.

This merger of scientific and spiritual insights about the power and glory of the divine feminine could be called Quantum Shaktism. We can use this concept to realize that there is unlimited potential, light, creativity and love within ourselves, gifted to us by the divine mother.

If we view the quantum superstring - this field of infinite possibility - as life-giving light energy, we realize it is the love that flows from the mother of the universe. She is what forms the oscillating waves, particles and patterns. She is the source of what creates this dimension from the ethers. Once her light enters this dimension, the male God energy then transmutes her light into form.

If we think of the divine mother Goddess as the source from which physical existence arises, we start to view reality more positively, more hopefully, as she represents the infinite possibilities that can spring into existence at any moment. The Shakti force is light, love, and creative life-giving energy that allows for new ideas, new thoughts, and new forms.

As we rediscover the goddess within, we unify our inner being to function in unison with all life. We are now not just rational, but intuitive beings; we are logical, and now, more creative; we can take action, yet we are able to detach and just enjoy "being," existing in peaceful contentment in connection with all that is.

> *The restatement of the feminine, both human and divine, is critical to our spiritual survival. Nothing is going to delay the Goddess's second coming, whether in the guise of Sophia, or any other form. As she emerges, so the imbalances of our culture will inevitably iron themselves out.*
> **–Laura Magdalene Eisenhower**

If thoughts are waveforms that affect the vibration of matter, then we are the ones who are collectively creating our reality. However, our personal effect on the environment may have been somewhat over stated, as it takes lengthy focused, sustained effort to manifest change at the individual level. Only when enough of us band together with unified loving intent will we truly be able to change the physical world. This shift could actually occur in an instant, once a critical mass of participants is achieved, as foretold by so many different belief systems.

9

A Balanced God Image

Simply put, regardless of whether you are a man or a woman, we can achieve a harmonious unity of these complementary opposite states within our spiritual, mental, and emotional being. Male energy is described as being concerned with causation, effecting change through action and outward effort. While female energy focuses on what is already resident in beingness. The male polarity within governs intellect, while the female governs intuition and imagination.

Within the male mind, we are blind to possibilities that do not yet exist, yet those who revere the goddess know that she provides the ability to create an entire new reality, just through the inspiration she sends to our hearts, minds, bodies, and souls - all we have to do is ask. So, connecting to the Goddess energy provides a knowing, an inner faith, that we will be provided for, as we use the God energy to move forward and take positive action in the real world.

Western society is now being improved by a return to a veneration of the Goddess. When we speak of God the Father, we ask for his blessing and guidance; but our image of him is still limited by assuming he is male. While the male image is seen as being able to provide and support, it lacks the magical, mysterious, intuitive creativity of the feminine. This is a mental trap of sorts as we become conditioned to only believe what we perceive and not to realize that we can also draw upon what is yet unformed in the ethers.

With Quantum Shaktism, the Goddess or divine mother is the source from which all things are created, and when we realize this, we recognize that all things are connected as well. This awareness automatically brings more realization of our interdependence, which brings more cooperation and peace.

In many Eastern cultures, the divine feminine has always been regarded not just as a secondary source of power but as the primal power. As previously mentioned, the Hindu beliefs, for example, maintain that it is the Shakti (feminine energy) that flows through our body and connects us all to each other and to nature. (This idea was beautifully portrayed in the recent movie *Avatar*). In Shaktism, devotional prayers and mantras are practiced to amplify the creative feminine energy and increase its power within us, whether we are male or female.

> *She supports life, re-birth, and new ideas, and new ways are entering the world to bring healing. The mother mind is what we all need to find within ourselves as men and women. She does not think linearly, she thinks sideways upwards and downwards, and she teaches us that we must FEEL what is going on. Do not listen, sense, do not think, feel.*
> -**Vusamazulu Credo Mutwa**

10

REALIZATIONS

The few simple ideas outlined in this chapter help explain why we exist and what life is all about; they capture the essence of what I have learned during several decades of spiritual study, metaphysical reflection, and open-minded searching for the ultimate truth through science, religion, philosophy, and history.

Eight important realizations about the true nature of reality and the purpose of this life:

1. We do not dissolve into nothing at death - We expand into everything

Part of our awareness is emanating from a higher, non-physical, un-manifest realm. This part of us is eternal, omniscient, and omnipresent. From that perspective, the experience of this life is just the blink of an eye. This world is almost not real in terms of what comprises the ultimate metaphysical reality, as our existence here is temporary. The eternal absolute reality is the real world. Consider this quote from the beginning of the globally popular book, *A Course In Miracles*:

Nothing real can be threatened, nothing unreal exists.

At first, I did not comprehend the idea being conveyed. Then, I recalled these few lines (non-sequential) from the Ribhu Gita, relating to the paradox of Brahman:

Line 19: *The Guru, indeed, does not exist; truly, there is no disciple. There being only Brahman alone, be of the certitude that there is no non-Self.*

Line 32: *I am Consciousness, and there is no non-Self. Be of this certitude. Thus, in brief, the definition of the Self has been told to you.*

Line 33. *By hearing this once, one becomes Brahman oneself*

Also, in the *Bhagavad Gita*, Krishna explains to Arjuna the eternal nature of the Atman, the ultimate and immortal Self. He explains to Arjuna that we must detach ourselves from the fleeting nature of the "I," which Krishna described as a fiction created by Avidya, meaning delusion or metaphysical ignorance. And that our true nature is that of Parabrahm (the Godhead itself or Bramha).

The ignorance of metaphysical knowledge is humanity's greatest predicament.

Modern science claims that consciousness arises from the brain. But the brain really could just be a transceiver for a consciousness that lives beyond time and space. Per the words of physicist Nassim Haramein, *"...looking for consciousness in the brain is like looking inside a radio for the announcer."* When you die, the radio goes out, and your consciousness becomes unable to tune in to the frequency of this dimension and level of vibration anymore. So if atheistic thinking with its fatalistic pessimism has gotten you depressed, know that this physical reality is not the only frequency level.

Why do we know? Because quantum physics has shown us that matter is emanating out of nowhere, out of nothing, from the void, yet it forms perfectly into manifestation. The void is just a wall, a barrier between levels, so this level is emanating from a higher level through the void. Quantum physics asserts that hidden formless dimensions are forming this one and that there is something behind all this.

> *As above, so below, as within so without, as the universe, so the soul.*
> **-Hermes Trismegistus**

The above quote implies that the higher, unmanifest realms are the real world - we came from there and will return there. Again, source consciousness is nonmaterial and trans-dimensional. Matter is just the slowest, lowest vibrational representation of source consciousness and is like a reflection that has temporarily solidified. Whether it's dark matter, the vacuum, the void, or a hidden undetected level, science has identified that at the quantum level something is in fact emanating from nothing and that there has to be a "something" to the nothing.

2. The reality of nothing

As I reflected on this idea of nothing being the source of everything, I remembered reading William Gray's book *Qabbalistic Concepts* in which he addresses the metaphysical shift in perception that is needed to grasp the paradox of creation:

> *Which was in the beginning, is now, and ever will be, amen? Because we cannot very well name the unnameable, most mystics agree to term it nothing. No thing. Zero. The cypher of*

infinity. 0. Let us think about this for a bit. Ideas of nothing frighten most ordinary Westerners. All they can think of is death, destruction, ruin, poverty, and the absolute worst of everything they can imagine. For the average materially-minded Westerner, "things" mean wealth, possessions, power, prosperity, all he wants out of life, while "no-thing" means exactly the reverse.

He finds it almost impossible to face the fact that physical death deprives him of all his "things" in a split second. He knows this well enough deep inside himself, but he would rather not confront it consciously. The last thing he wants to admit is that his 'things' will only last a lifetime, whereas his "nothing" is going to last forever. The mystic, on the other hand, takes an opposite view. He is interested in whatever exists eternally because he realizes it must be far more important than temporary and transient things, however fascinating they may be in the moment.

If "nothing" or 0 is the symbol for what he considers to be true "spiritual solidity," then he means to make relationships with this, and if possible, discover his own immortal identity therein. Something "deeper than deep" in himself tells him to do so, even though he may not know the whys and hows on the surface of his consciousness....Sometimes we call it "No-thing," sometimes "God," but probably the most acceptable definition so far is the old Rosicrucian one of Perfect Peace Profound (P.P.P.). That is what Western mystics and magicians mean when they think of nothing, a state of perfection, of peace and of profundity utterly beyond any human comprehension.
-William Gray

As I reflected on the deep wisdom revealed by the teachings of the Qabala, I remembered that I had met a psychic named Sean from Salem, Massachusetts, who had told me a few years before that William Gray would be an important source of information for me. Sean was also the first to tell me that I would be a writer. At the time, I laughed and said I had no plans to ever write anything.

To summarize, the riddle of creation has been solved, all realities are formed out of the one great super consciousness. You are not you, i.e., you are pure consciousness itself.

3. We need to balance our God image to include the Goddess.

I equate the Goddess to the quantum superstring itself. She is pure potential and infinite possibility - that which creates life. This Shakti force precedes the Shiva - that which manifests into form. Balancing our God image to include a Goddess or divine feminine creatrix automatically helps us shift into a heart-based consciousness and an awareness of our oneness with each other and all life. And, whether you are a man or a woman, raising up the Goddess does not mean we push aside the sacred male. Shiva and Shakti uphold the circle of life equally by maintaining a perfect balance of each polarity. Consider the icon of Radha, as she represents the image of creation's greatest accomplishment: human woman. The leela (playful dance) of love between Krishna and Radha captures the joy of life itself. Just like the archetype of Shiva and Shakti represent the interplay of consciousness and energy, the essence of creation.

4. Divine intervention is possible - through ourselves.

Life is a vibrating possibility up to the last millisecond.
-Carl Johan Calleman

How is divine intervention possible? Through ourselves. We are the conduit for higher trans-dimensional energies via our thoughts and feelings, especially when guided by loving intent, as that is the means to start acting and living together in love and oneness.

Utopia awaits - it's really possible.

If you ask the God or Goddess, the higher power, the creator, or the matrix to assist, he/she/it will. But keep in mind that while you can ask for an answer to your prayers, just don't tell the Godhead exactly how to answer them. How you will be helped will be in accordance with your divine life's mission, your soul purpose, and not necessarily the needs of your ego-mind-body complex as you want them. Technically, you are helping yourself, as you are also the Godly source-consciousness which assists and sustains us all, but that assistance will manifest in a way that continues to teach you.

Spiritual growth is a process requiring work, determination, and focus. That's where metaphysical reflection is helpful, to keep you aware and awakened to your soul purpose, your reason for being.

Following deep meditation and prayer, I was able to connect with the creator long enough to have my life's mission revealed to me, which is to share ideas, observations, and insights about all matters metaphysical to inspire others and to proffer hope. For me, writing about spiritual information is not just a labor of love - it's an expression of what I am, not who I am. It is a fundamental need to tell the world what I have seen, felt, sensed, and learned about the higher worlds or hidden levels.

Divine intervention could be thought of as a force that powers the law of attraction here in the physical. Yet real-world success requires hard work and focused action to steadily achieve a pre-defined goal. The hardest part of my spiritual journey has been to stay grounded, keep it real, and get life done. I am on my way to learning how to balance living in both worlds. I feel we are all getting divine intervention, globally, via an expanded consciousness and awareness, a loving vibration or energy which is growing in the hearts and minds of all humans on this earth.

5. Heart-based consciousness is the key to manifesting a new positive reality.

Thoughts are things. Feelings are vibrations. Thoughts come and go and drift in and out. Only when a thought is focused and backed by feeling can it manifest. The Hopi prophecy reveals that we are entering a time of great change in consciousness that shifts us from head to heart:

> *Nothing living will go untouched, here or in the heavens. The way through this time, it is said, is to be found in our hearts, and re-uniting with our spiritual self. Getting simple and returning to living with and upon the Earth in harmony with her creatures.*
> **-Hopi Blue Star Prophecy**

We need to stay positive and just start doing what we want to achieve, while sending heavenly light and divine love out from the heart. This positive, divine energy changes this world for the better and creates possibilities for positive action and events. Imagine a loving world, where everyone has everything they need, emotionally, mentally, and physically.

The meaning of this life is the evolution of consciousness, and when it's guided by a loving heart, our experience of this reality seems to flow much better. Thinking with the heart is the key to a higher, spiritually minded, loving existence. We can't go to the higher worlds with negative emotions and thought vibrations. We need to heal character defects, karmic situations and traumas, and get rid of negative thinking and limiting beliefs.

Even though I do not currently have the economic success of my earlier years, I am now so incredibly wealthy in spirit and heart. I am 100 times more joyful and serene than I ever thought possible when I look back at the state of mental depression I experienced then.

My spiritual name, Sriman Das, means "he who serves the mother of the world" or "he who carries Lakshmi on his chest." Lakshmi is the goddess of fortune, and she has given me friendships and associations of great depth and beauty. That is the true wealth you can glean from this world; that is real success, spiritually speaking. Thanks to Sripad Bhaktivedanta Sadhu Maharaja, for his blessing of my spiritual name.

6. The oneness of consciousness.

You are not your body and mind; you are pure consciousness itself; and that consciousness connects with prime creator and all beings:

> *The operation of consciousness has created the 'apparition' called 'me'.*
> **-Sri Mooji**

> *That, within which even silence is heard; before perception arose. Which, itself, perceives perceiving. That concept-less and Immutable Being-ness. That alone Is. -That we are.*
> **-Sri Mooji**

Mooji's message is that during deep meditation we can become aware of the consciousness that observes the body mind, that which watches. My interpretation of this is that I am not really me – completely anyway. This life is a game being played out by the higher self-awareness, our soul essence from somewhere else.

> *Who is it that's aware that I'm thinking?*
> **-Jim Carrey**

Mooji and Carrey both make the point that we have a higher awareness and that we can step outside of ourselves and become one with the all unified consciousness itself.

Further, if an interconnection exists between all-sentient, self-aware conscious beings everywhere in the universe, then love for one another is actually a solution to resolving our problems in this world, as the current Dalai Lama, Tenzin Gyatso said:

> *Suffering begins with the illusion of separateness, the myth of individuality.*

While modern science is now just beginning to study the relationship between consciousness and matter, a paradigm shift in thinking is now under way that should bring us deeper insights:

> *When we talk about the power of "invisible forces" such as belief, to many scientists, we've crossed the line that separates science from everything else. Maybe it's precisely because this line is so hard to define that we often learn about it only after we've already crossed it. My personal belief is that by relaxing the boundaries that have traditionally kept science and spirituality separate, we'll ultimately find the power of a greater wisdom. With the new discoveries showing that consciousness affects everything from the cells of our bodies to the atoms of our world, belief is clearly at the forefront of that exploration today. Interestingly, it has also become the place where science,*

faith, and even spirituality seem to be finding common ground.
-Gregg Braden, *The Spontaneous Healing of Belief*

Gregg Braden is one of the great thought leaders of the paradigm shift that is unifying science and spirituality. I too believe that the deepest truths ought to be able to be described and communicated by either method of thought.

7. Acceptance of the balance of life

My pursuit of spiritual information and studies of the metaphysical are helping me to function better in the physical and allowing me to enjoy the ride as well. While researching what others have gleaned from the *Bhagavad Gita*, I happened upon the words of Alexandra Muller Arboleda. She shares some very practical spiritual insights in a blog post about the *Bhagavad Gita* that seem to distill the essence of some key principles of Hinduism and Buddhism which I also have come to know and live by:

Surrender the fruits of your actions.

Find contentment with the journey you are on regardless of outcomes, even when the walls are crumbling around you and the earth is cracking beneath your feet.

Do not expect or fear anything.

Expectation and fear limit our possibilities. Accept the dualities of life:

Be at ease in pleasure and pain, in honor and disgrace. Do not rejoice in good fortune nor lament bad fortune. Free yourself from desire and anger.

Accept the equanimity of life: When you see all beings as equal in suffering and in joy, when you are rooted in the oneness of all beings, you cannot love or hate because it is all part of the same thing. Put in other words, love your enemy as yourself. Refuse to speak badly about those who hurt you or your enemies. Limiting your speech will limit your negative thoughts and eventually allow you to forgive in your heart and mind as well. Then you can approach your enemies with kindness and empathy.

The wise are free of attachments and act for the well-being of the whole world.

Free yourself from being overly attached to things. Love without needing or possessing. Hope and dream without being attached to the outcome of your dreams. Think about what you can give to the world rather than your own problem.
-Alexandra Muller Arboleda[11]

Arboleda's insights relay the idea of our interconnection to the one true self and the need to be aware of our dual awareness as we walk the earth and interact with others. That higher awareness can keep us in a non-attached state of loving compassion. And, as we reflect upon the impermanence of ourselves and this world, the paradox that non-attachment from this world allows us to better experience it comes to the fore. We have to live and abide, function, and do our duty in the physical, yet we need to keep an awareness of our true metaphysical nature. This life is a fleeting instance, yet every moment has enormous value and meaning to our eternal soul(s).

8. Maintain spiritual sovereignty.

While spiritual philosophers have shown us the value of overcoming the limits of the ego by honoring the Godhead, we need to balance this with a caution about giving away too much of our personal power to a religion or spiritual belief system. I feel that we can all connect directly with creator, with no need of any intermediary. If we worship or ask assistance from a master, guide, angel, or god/goddess, do we know who or what that being really is? Are we blindly following some entity or being based on the experience of others? On the other hand, there are people of beauty and integrity, as well as valid, unifying mystical truths in many spiritual teachings and paths. You must therefore endeavor to divine what is true and correct for you, in the sacred space of the heart.

Some paths ask you to surrender your power to the guru and treat the guru as God, but I also caution you on this and echo two great masters who I greatly respect for their beliefs on worship. Yogi Satyam insisted that we all need to connect directly to creator. And the current Dalai Lama insists that we should always follow our own heartfelt intuition when it aligns with common sense. There are certainly guides, gurus and masters in my personal practice, but for me, I ask that any worship, honoring, or prayer be directed to prime creator itself. When mantras or prayers are directed to individual gods, goddesses or angels, realize that each just represents an archetypal state of being or energy. I have simplified my mantra practice as well and now only focus on bringing divine love of creator into the world.

The secular humanist movement of recent years has served to expose the dangers of religion. Religions are a set of tenets based on other people's experience that sometimes ask followers to believe without much attention to science, logic, and reason. And yet all religious orders feature people of great inner beauty, personal integrity, and true compassionate devotion to serving others.

Here we confront another paradox. Religion contains some philosophic and spiritual principles and ideas that heal the world, yet when its beliefs and principles become too outdated or rigid, they can cause destruction in the world through ignorance, fear, and manipulation. So, instead of worshiping, seek to connect with the higher power with love in your heart and respect and appreciation for all life, everywhere.

11

THE ACTUAL HEARTSPACE PORTAL

We can bring divine love, or what I call Quantum Love into the world via the Heartspace Portal - the sacred chamber that houses the soul. In ancient vedic lore, there is a description of the *Hrit Padma*, which is one and the same with the idea of the Heartspace Portal:

> *In the very center of the human organism, we find the Hridaya Padana Chakra or the* Hrit Padma. *The Hrit is within the Anahata Chakra, in this temple lies the undifferentiated singularity in the pericarp of the lotus flower, at the core of*

which is a yin yang dual torus field. In short, the Hridaya Padana Chakra contains the Hrit Padma or the Hrit Lotus. The dweller of the lotus of the heart Chakra is described in the Brahma Upanishad....all deities, all pranavayus and prana, and the divine light dwell in the Hrit Chakra. All these are in the heart which is in the nature of consciousness. In the Gita Saa it is stated: the Hrit Lotus has 8 petals, and inside the pericarp is the sun. Inside the sun is the moon, inside the moon is fire, and inside fire is a radiance, wherein there is a seat which is ornamented with jewels, which is very bright. On this seat, the Lord God Narayan is seated. This is the seat of the universal self....Concentrate on the all pervading perfectly pure being within the hollow of the Hrit Padma.

The Garuda Purana confirms, the Atma, the self is situated in the Hrit Padma or Hrit Pundari (heart lotus). The divine form of Narayan as Krishna, is within the fully bloomed 8 petaled lotus.... This is where the Atma (human soul) an the undifferentiated self arise from, the secret name of Atman is the truth of all truths. The Hridaya, which is like the bud of a Lotus, has a space turned downwards in relation to it (this is reminscent of a Torus field), where lies an infinitesimal void, the Sukshma (Subtle) Sushira (Hollow), the place where is situated, the whole, the all, the one.
-Shaktipat Seer

(Para-phrased from *Shabdabrahman*[12]: *The Divine Vibration Video* (A Documentary On Ancient Vedic Science For A New Age)

It is interesting that Shaktipat Seer references the torus field, for it is a fundamental geometric structure found in all aspects of material existence and is similar to the Mer-Ka-Ba energy field (chariot of ascension), as well as the human aura. Having practiced the Mer-Ka-Ba meditation, I have felt the effect of activating my light body (astral body or soul), and I have felt the energy field around my body, centered in the heart. Simply put, creator itself resides in the sacred space of our heart(s).

The Hrit Padma is the Heartspace Portal. It is a portal to heaven, and therefore the conduit through which we bring divinity into manifestation in this world.

> *Divine happiness, even the tiniest particle of a grain of it, never leaves one again; and when one attains to the essence of things and finds one's Self–this is supreme happiness. When it is found, nothing else remains to be found; the sense of want will not awaken anymore, and the heart's torment will be stilled forever.*
> -**Sri Anandamayi Ma**

Enter the Heartspace Portal

The technique of entering the Heartspace Portal is so simple and is more effective the more it is practiced. Here is a suggested technique that we can all implement for ourselves and share with others to change the world one heart at a time:

Meditative Version

Dear self/selves. You can step into a sacred chamber that really is a doorway to heaven. In that space you find total peace and joy; you feel a divine love from a higher power, and you bring that love into your life, your world, and your space, now.

- Put your left hand on your heart, and place your right hand over your left. As you hold your hands over your heart, close your eyes and feel the love you have for yourself and all beings and creatures, everywhere in the physical universe and also in the heavenly realms.

- Touch your tongue to the roof of your mouth to open a connection from your brain to your heart.

Imagine divine love as a white light streaming down from the higher worlds. Imagine that this divine light energy enters at the center of this universe, then, visualize it streaming down from there as it enters through the top of your head and into your heart. At the same time, visualize a light coming from the center of the earth, up through your feet and into your heart. For in the heart is where you balance the worlds.

- ✎ When both sources of light meet in your sacred heartspace, send this combined light-stream out from your heart and through your hands, forming a bubble of light around you in a glowing sphere. Affirm that this light only allows or attracts positive beautiful experiences, thoughts, ideas, people, places, and things into your life.

- ✎ Visualize this bubble of light connecting with the other bubbles of light formed by all the other people on the earth, as they too possess this same light.

- ✎ Imagine that this connected grid of bubbles of light expands to form one big bubble over the whole earth.

- ✎ Then say out loud or to yourself:

> *I am love, I am light, I am one with all life. Heaven on earth is here now. Infinite possibilities of love, happiness, abundance, and peace are now manifesting into my life and into the world, for the greatest good of all, from the Hrit Padma, my sacred heartspace.*

Short version

Use this shortened version when you are on the go, out in the world, at work, at play or wherever:

- ✎ Put your left hand on your heart, and place your right hand over your left.

- ✎ Close your eyes say out loud or to yourself:

> *I am love, I am light, I am one with all life. Heaven on earth is here now.*

Mantra version

A third, simple option is to use a mantra. I use the Om Prema, a standard Hindu mantra, as one of my own daily meditations, but I do not chant it to any particular god or goddess. Om Prema is divine love, or what I call Quantum Love, which I visualize as the light emanating from the quantum superstring.

Om Parama Prema Rupaya Namaha[13]

(It is highly recommended to repeat the above mantra at least 108 times.) 108 repetitions is known as a "round" for the 108 beads that are contained on a standard Hindu or Buddhist set of mala beads. The more rounds you can do, the better. On busy days, I may only do a round or two, but at some point in the week, I set aside time to do 10 rounds or 1080 repetitions at a sitting.

Meaning: *Oh Manifestation of Divine Love, I honor you.*

This mantra requests the manifestation of Divine Love in a person's life, in a form the person can comprehend. From experience I can say that the more it is recited, the more it brings an abiding sense of peace and contentment. It is my way of returning to a contemplative mindset when worldly affairs start to separate me from my soul. While chanting this mantra, it is said that one can have an experience or vision (Dharshan) of the Divine.

Om - *Supreme Vibration*
Parama - *Pure*
Prema - *Love*
Rupaya - *Manifestation*
Namaha - *I honor you*

A note about mantras and Sanskrit. Mantras in this ancient language are effective because of their vibrational effect on our entire being. I feel they are a spiritual technology of sorts. You do not need to be a Hindu to use and apply the power of mantras in your life. The vibrational effect will positively affect anyone who says the mantra with sincerity.

Performing the mantras and meditation exercises to activate the HeartSpace Portal, especially in groups, will get more and more people to activate their higher consciousness and connection to source. To facilitate both individual and group enlightenment, there is a free printed handout with all versions of the mediation, available at: www.quantumlove.net/heartspace-portal-meditation. You can also purchase the MP3 guided version there as well.

12

BRINGING HEAVEN TO EARTH NOW

My studies of mystical spirituality taught me that healing and loving the self heals the world. That's why the idea of using the Heartspace Portal which resides within each of us, is a beautiful technique, a simple way for us all to achieve a Utopian experience, together, in this present reality.

Sound impossible? It's not.

All we need to do is get enough people to use this technique and embrace this idea, for it is an easily understandable means or method to shift out of the fear, the separation, and the division we experience here in the temporal world of duality and shift up to a fifth-dimensional unified higher state of consciousness and loving awareness.

When we make a comparison between the heart and brain from a spiritual perspective, we find that the things we create or attract solely with the power of our rational brain can bring a corresponding karma because causative mental emotions often arise from the ego. Because the ego lives in abject service to self, often without the consideration of the needs of others (especially when influenced by fear), a commensurate amount of negative karma can accompany the creation of what we think is a positive circumstance. However, manifesting reality from the heart obviates any karmic negative consequence, as the heart only brings into being that which is for the highest and best good of all.

The heart is predisposed to consider the needs of others before the desires of the self. This is why the heart is considered to be the spiritual conduit for divine energies that flow into our world from the higher realms. If we think of love as a malleable energy, which we can infuse into our lives to positively affect things, we realize that divine love energy is the key to vibrational manifestation and the means by which matter itself can be altered, sometimes even miraculously.

Einstein said that what makes us God-like is our compassion. Without it, we would just be robots. Our real power, therefore, does not lie in our computer-like brain capacity; rather, it dwells in our ability to generate feelings. Feelings are far more effective at moving energy than thought. A thought is only a catalyst to evoke a feeling, and those who study and apply the law of attraction successfully to life know that feelings drive the transformation of reality.

Scientifically, in terms of energy, it has been shown that the heart actually emits thousands of times more electromagnetic energy than the brain. In units of electromagnetic energy, the heart emits 5,000 femotesla[14] units versus only 100 femotesla units emitted by the brain.

Rupert Sheldrake, a biochemist, developed the theory that an invisible, morphogenic energy field exists around us that he described as influencing the pattern or form of things. This collective energy field is thought to affect the creation, growth, and function of living organisms, and to some extent, the effect of our consciousness on the surrounding environment.

In eastern philosophy, Daoists (those who study the Dao, or Tao) call this field the unitive field, a nonphysical matrix that connects all minds with all matter. It is thought that the interaction of our consciousness with this field affects which people, places, events, and circumstances will enter our reality and their predisposed response to us.

Again, we all create our own "reality tunnel" with our emotions and mindset, as our consciousness reacts with the unified field. As the human heart is the generator of our feeling state, it is the primary transceiver for creating or attracting whatever occurs in our individual lives. The sum of our individual realities is creating our collective future.

If we can learn to live in love, oneness, and cooperation, we can shift up to a higher, better reality together. We just need to attain a critical mass of enough enlightened souls who hold the space and the peaceful vibration necessary to allow everyone else to follow.

13

Quantum Love

In times of old, we asked the Gods, spirits, and guides to assist us. In this modern age, we need to recognize the existence of the unmanifest level that shapes and forms our reality via the one universal super-consciousness. From this unmanifest level comes the power of divine love energy - the Om Prema that emanates directly from prime creator.

We can use this power to heal, to assist, and to serve the whole of humanity and all of God's creatures. This is how and why we all really do have God-like power. The philosophy of Quantum Love is that we can all bring the Om Prema into the world via the Heartspace Portal, or the sacred space of the heart.

Quantum Love is the Om Prema, a transformational power which we humans can use to positively change ourselves along with the people, places, and things that manifest in our individual lives. And by doing so, we will automatically change the entire world for the better via the Bodhisattva effect. We can all live a life filled with love, peace, and harmony, as soon as we realize that we are the ones we are waiting for. We can all co-create a better reality using our capacity for compassion, empathy, caring, and community.

Religion teaches unconditional love, a good and necessary attitude, which has brought more oneness and peace to the world. Divine love is a resource, and we humans have the unique gift in being able to transmute this reality and bring heaven to earth. Quantum Love is the malleable fabric of heaven that we can ALL weave into the world to benefit and uplift all of creation.

I have worked on healing myself from the inside out, asking source consciousness, the prime creator or Godhead itself, to send higher frequencies of divine love and light into my heart, mind, body, and soul. This process has slowly transformed my consciousness to the point where I have begun to develop a feeling of cosmic awareness, and, as a result, an abiding inner peace.

Remember, daily meditation and the achievement of non-thought will accelerate this ability. You will begin to realize that everything is just energy and that bringing in these higher dimensional vibrations of love will start to change your life for the better. People, places, and things will start to arrange themselves differently. This process is slow, but it is steady as long you focus on maintaining a high level of vibration, intention, awareness, and love.

We change the world by changing ourselves - slowly. And when we can come together as a group, with positive loving divine intent, we will rapidly transform our civilization for the better. This is about critical mass and the synergistic effect of the power that spiritual love in this world can be brought to bear. It is the magical power we human beings possess and need to start practicing.

Regarding the nature of consciousness and being, I believe that our individual consciousness is not completely ours because we are not really who we think we are. We are all parts of something far greater; that is the truth; that you and I are the Atman, one and the same as part of the all pervasive self. We are eternally metaphysical and only temporarily physical. That sense of I and YOU, as separateness, is an illusion. Look at others through the eyes of empathy. It's time to care and awaken to the idea of bringing divine love into the world via the quantum field. Individually and collectively, we can bring heaven to Earth NOW.

Pranam,
Mark Collins
Sriman Das

Further Reading

Topics, great thinkers and authors who provide wonderful insights and are worth your attention include:

12 Step Recovery system(s)
A Course in Miracles
Advaita Vedanta
Alan Watts
AMMA
Anandamayi Ma
Ayurveda
Barbara Marciniak
BIll Hicks
Bhagavad Gita
Black Elk
Dion Fortune
Druidic Spiritual Lore
Drunvalo Melchizedek
Eckankar
Edgar Cayce
Ellie Crystal
Gnosticism
Gurdjieff
Haidakhan Babaji
Henry David Thoreau
Hermeticism
Huna
Integrated Energy Therapy
Jiddu Krishnamurti
Kabbalah
Kadampa Buddhism
Kashmiri Shaivism
Kriyayoga
Kundalini Yoga
Lynn McTaggart

Madame Blavatsky
Maharishi Mahesh
Manly P. Hall
Mary Baker Eddy
Mary Magdalene
Matt Kahn
Max Heindel
Meditative Yoga
Meher Baba
Mooji
Mother Teresa
Native American spirituality
Neale Donald Walsch
Neem Karoli Baba
Nikola Tesla
Neo-Pagan ideals
Nisargadatta Maharaj
Neuro Linguistic Programming
Quakerism
Rabindrinath Tagore
Ralph Waldo Emerson
Robert Adams
Rosicrucianism
Rudolf Steiner
Rupert Sheldrake
Secular Humanism
Siddha Yoga
Sri Aurobindo
Swami Vivekananda
Terence McKenna
The Hare Krishna Movement
The Kybalion
The Ribhu Gita
Theosophism
Unitarian Universalism

Wicca
Yogi Bhajan
Yogiraj Gurunath Siddhanath

REFERENCES

1- Sadhana - (Hinduism) one of a number of spiritual practices or disciplines which lead to perfection, these being contemplation, asceticism, worship of a god, and correct living.

2- Samadhi - Hinduism, Buddhism. The highest stage in meditation, in which a person experiences oneness with the universe.

3- Andrea Tteja - Yogini at: www.infin8space.com

4- Meher Baba quote - Avatarmeherbaba.org

5- The Swami Vivekananda, David Bohm and the Chandogya Upanishad I.9.1 - excerpts taken from: *The Self-Actualizing Cosmos: The Akasha Revolution in Science and Human Consciousness* published by Inner Traditions at: http://realitysandwich.com/218055/akasha/

6- Dr Amit Goswami on Coast to Coast AM www.coasttocoastam.com/guest/goswami-amit/41632

7- Eckankar – a new age spiritual path about connecting to the light and sound of God, with reference to the idea of higher spiritual worlds or "planes of existence" that was inspired by the Punjabi Sant Mat tradition.

8- Information on the Moebius and Srinivasa Ramanujan taken from: theprophecychronicles.com/100-year-old-deathbed-dreams-of-mathematician-proved-true

9 - See: learner.org/courses/physics/visual ADDED

10- Definition of Adi Parashakti taken from: tswiki.net/mywiki/index.php?title=Aditi

11- Source of Alexandra Muller Arboleda quote(s):
http://yoganonymous.
com/8-things-i-learned-from-the-bhagavad-gita/

12- Shabdabrahman: The Divine Vibration" by
Shaktipat Seer: https://www.youtube.com/watch?v=-0GXQlJMx-
NA&list=PL6E0BF2D0D56DFC5E

Author's note: This book came to me in parts and pieces and
not in sequential order, yet it all makes perfect sense to me now
as I realize it is now complete. Why? Because I did not discover
or realize that the Hrit Padma was the Sanskrit word for the
Heartspace Portal that I was looking for until after I had written most of this book. When I discovered the Hrit Padma and
Hridaya Padana Chakra information from the "Shabdabrahman:
The Divine Vibration" video by Shaktipat Seer, I knew this was
the last piece of the puzzle I was looking for. Thank you for your
beautiful and eloquent video production that was so moving and
inspiring Shaktipat Seer!

The idea for this type if simple exercise was partly inspired by
some of the ideas presented in The Messenger, a book by Klaus
Joehle, who recommends forming a bubble of white light and
love within the heart, then sending it out ahead of you into the
world. Much metta and love to you Klaus!!

13- The source reference for the Om Parama Prema Rupaya
Namaha mantra:
http://www.healingsound.org/Mantras.aspx?id=92Mantras.
aspx?id=92)

14- Heart and Brain femotesla information from:
https://www.heartmath.org/

ABOUT THE AUTHOR

Mark Collins, Sriman Das

To seek, to learn, to grow, in spirit and in love. This is why we are alive. This is our life's mission. As a spiritual explorer I have spent the last four decades of my life studying many spiritual and religious belief systems. I've analyzed many things metaphysical, as well as all things paranormal and unexplained. What I have I gleaned? What is my message? It is all one, we are all one, one with each other, and the infinity of existence itself. And the best way to make that infinite connection real is to practice it in our lives caring for each other and ourselves.

About Me:
Freelance writer - Insights and commentary about any and all information that is enlightening and serves the cause of global enlightenment, peace and freedom for all.

Columnist - "Metaphysical View" - *Intrepid Magazine* - 2010 to 2015

Columnist - Spirituality Almanac column - *TAPS Paramagazine* - 2005 to 2010 (A fan magazine for the popular Discovery Channel Series – *Ghost Hunters*)

Radio co-host - www.blogtalkradio.com/hearthealers

Website: www.QuantumLove.net

Healer:
Originator of the Samasta Method for energy healing
Reiki Master (Also trained in Integrated Energy Therapy and Huna)
Neuro Linguistic Programming practitioner

SEMINAR AND WORKSHOP

In addition to my healing work and writing, I offer a basic class and a one day mini-seminar.

For information on attending, contact me at: srimandas@gmail.com Or contact me via the contact form at: www.Quantumlove.net

1 DAY SEMINAR

Quantum Love (Spiritual Metaphysics)

The Quantum Love seminar shares deep insights and truths about the true nature of reality, our consciousness, and being from a spiritual perspective. Enlightening, liberating, and optimistically reassuring, the seminar is a blend of the spiritual and metaphysical, with deep insights into why we exist, what this life is about, and most importantly, how to "walk the walk" of your spirituality, in harmony with your true life's purpose.

1 DAY WORKSHOP

Meditation Basics - Awareness of Oneness - Chakras, Mudras & Mantras

A superb intro to all the basic components of a meditative practice which also features basic pranayama breathing techniques. This is not a yoga class; it is a meditation class featuring principles from meditative aspects of various yoga and other systems.

A deeper exploration of the chakras with instruction and a look at their meanings: how to balance our physical, mental, and emotional aspects of being with a spiritually guided meditation that features sound healing with Himalayan crystal bowl tones and soothing music in the solfeggio frequency range.

IMAGE CREDITS